SEARCHING FOR
ALIEN LIFE

by Todd Kortemeier

12 STORY LIBRARY

www.12StoryLibrary.com

12-Story Library is an imprint of Peterson Publishing Company and Press Room Editions.

Produced for 12-Story Library by Red Line Editorial

Photographs ©: NASA, cover, 1, 10, 13, 21, 22, 28; Iryna1/Shutterstock Images, 4; Turtix/Shutterstock Images, 5; NRAO/AUI, 7; Hui Yang/University of Illinois OD/Nursery of New Stars/NASA, 8, 29; Paulo Afonso/Shutterstock Images, 9; NASA/JHUAPL/SwRI, 11; NASA/JPL-Caltech/SETI Institute, 12; Tischenko Irina/Shutterstock Images, 14; Kenneth Keifer/Shutterstock Images, 15; NASA/JPL-Caltech/ MSSS, 16; Malin Space Science Systems, MGS, JPL, NASA, 17; Mopic/Shutterstock Images, 18; Kim Shiflett/NASA, 19; NASA/JPL-Caltech, 20, 23, 36; David Higginbotham/MSFC/NASA, 24; NASA/ESA/ Leiden University/the HUDF09 Team, 25; Matej Kastelic/Shutterstock Images, 27

Library of Congress Cataloging-in-Publication Data
Names: Kortemeier, Todd, 1986- author.
Title: Searching for alien life / by Todd Kortemeier.
Description: North Mankato, MN : 12-Story Library, [2017] | Series: Science
    frontiers | Audience: Grades 4 to 6. | Includes bibliographical
    references and index.
Identifiers: LCCN 2016007566 (print) | LCCN 2016012137 (ebook) | ISBN
    9781632353801 (library bound : alk. paper) | ISBN 9781632353979 (pbk. :
    alk. paper) | ISBN 9781621435211 (hosted ebook)
Subjects: LCSH: Search for Extraterrestrial Intelligence (Study group :
    U.S.)--Juvenile literature. | Life on other planets--Juvenile literature.
    | Interstellar communication--Juvenile literature. | Outer
    space--Exploration--Juvenile literature.
Classification: LCC QB54 .K567 2017 (print) | LCC QB54 (ebook) | DDC
    576.8/39--dc23
LC record available at http://lccn.loc.gov/2016007566

Printed in the United States of America
Mankato, MN
May, 2016

Access free, up-to-date content on this topic plus a full digital version of this book. Scan the QR code on page 31 or use your school's login at 12StoryLibrary.com.

Table of Contents

People Have Scanned the Skies for Centuries 4

SETI Starts the Search for Intelligent Life 6

Radio Telescopes Are Always Listening 8

Spacecraft Carry Messages 10

NASA Leads the Search for Life 12

Alien Life May Be Basic 14

Rovers Look for Martians 16

Exoplanets Could Be Other Earths 18

NASA Hopes to Return Soil from Mars 20

Manned Mission to Mars: The Next Giant Leap 22

Bigger Telescopes Might Spot Life 24

The Chemical Laptop Is a Space Laboratory 26

Fact Sheet 28

Glossary 30

For More Information 31

Index 32

About the Author 32

People Have Scanned the Skies for Centuries

People have long looked at the sky and wondered what's up there. The ancient Greeks imagined other planets held different life-forms. In the 1600s, people wrote stories about what it would be like to visit other worlds. These stories have been written ever since. Aliens have been featured in many books, movies, and television shows.

Italian scientist Galileo Galilei made many discoveries about the solar system using early telescopes.

Scientists began to see planets in more detail as telescopes advanced. An astronomer in 1894 believed he saw canals on Mars. The idea that there is intelligent

THE WAR OF THE WORLDS

In 1938, a radio version of *The War of the Worlds* aired. The story is not real. Aliens from Mars invade Earth in the story. Many people did not know the program was not real. Radio stations received many calls from scared listeners.

6,743
UFO sightings in the United States in 2015 according to the National UFO Reporting Center.

life on other planets continues to excite people today. Technology has advanced to allow scientists to see farther and farther.

One major incident that got people interested in aliens took place in 1947. An unidentified object crashed near Roswell, New Mexico. People thought they had seen an alien spacecraft. The US Air Force assured people it was just a balloon used for observing the weather. But the event started a new wave of curiosity. People continue to report seeing unidentified flying objects (UFOs) in the skies.

- People have thought about life on other planets for thousands of years.
- Aliens have been a part of popular culture since the 1600s.
- Early telescopes allowed people to see other planets and to wonder what is on them.
- A mysterious crash in New Mexico in 1947 excited people about the chance of alien visitors.

SETI Starts the Search for Intelligent Life

For a long time, astronomers were able to see other planets but had no way to see whether anything lived on them. That changed in 1959. Two men came up with a different way of looking for life. Giuseppe Cocconi and Philip Morrison wrote about using radio waves to communicate across space. An astronomer named Frank Drake tried this method in 1960.

Drake turned an 85-foot (26-m) antenna toward two stars approximately the size of the sun. The antenna did not pick up a signal, but his method inspired others. The Search for Extraterrestrial Intelligence (SETI) was born.

Drake created the Drake Equation in 1961. It is used to estimate how many planets in the Milky Way galaxy might hold intelligent life. The equation considers the number of stars likely to have orbiting planets. It also considers how many of these might hold life.

Solving the Drake Equation would give humans an estimate of how many other civilizations in our galaxy might be able to communicate through space. But the Drake

160 billion
Estimated number of planets in the Milky Way galaxy.

- SETI began in 1959.
- Two men came up with the idea of using radio waves to search for life in space.
- Frank Drake did the first SETI experiment in 1960.
- Drake also created the Drake Equation. It outlines the conditions necessary for intelligent life.

Frank Drake used the Howard E. Tatel Radio Telescope in West Virginia to scan for signals.

Equation is not yet solvable. We do not know enough about our galaxy to solve it. The equation outlines the conditions needed for life. It currently helps SETI scientists know what to search for.

The SETI Institute was founded in 1984. It now has more than 130 employees searching for life in space. The institute has worked with many organizations, including the National Aeronautics and Space Administration (NASA).

SETI@HOME

With SETI@home, anyone can be a part of the search for life in space. This program uses people's home computers when people are not using them. Scientists at the University of California use that extra power. Having more computers means they can search more parts of space. A bunch of computers together equals one supercomputer. It increases SETI's ability to search for life.

Radio Telescopes Are Always Listening

Most people are familiar with telescopes people look through. But SETI uses a different kind of telescope called a radio telescope. This device is not used to see. Radio telescopes pick up radio waves. Some of these waves are natural. Planets give off heat that can be picked up as radio waves. But some radio waves could be from alien communication. These waves would be very faint by the time they got to Earth. A cell phone signal is billions of times stronger.

Radio telescopes used to be able to listen for only one signal at a time. Modern ones can scan the skies for many signals. This means these telescopes can pick up a lot of detail. But they also pick up a lot of unimportant waves. It's up to the

Radio telescopes detect waves that are not visible, but the waves they detect can be represented in real photos.

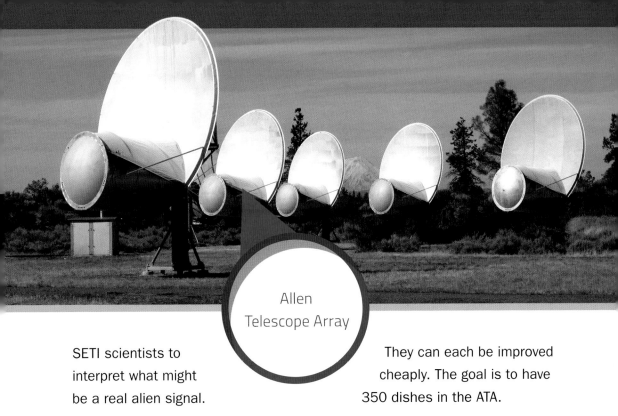

Allen
Telescope Array

SETI scientists to interpret what might be a real alien signal.

SETI uses a lot of telescopes. Some are very large. The SETI Institute uses the Allen Telescope Array (ATA) in Northern California. The array's first stage was finished in 2007 with 42 telescopes. It operates with that number today. The ATA allows SETI non-stop access to telescopes. Otherwise, they would have to borrow those owned by governments and universities.

Before the ATA, most SETI observations were made by huge, expensive dishes. But it was hard to upgrade the dishes. Dozens of smaller dishes working together can detect just as much as one big one.

They can each be improved cheaply. The goal is to have 350 dishes in the ATA.

20
Diameter, in feet (6.1 m), of each telescope at the ATA.

- SETI uses a type of telescope that listens for radio waves.
- SETI scientists interpret signals for signs of alien life.
- The SETI Institute uses 42 telescopes at the Allen Telescope Array in California.
- The ATA is planned to have 350 total dishes when completed.

Spacecraft Carry Messages

As humans explore more of space, the chances of finding alien life go up, if it exists. Probes have now gone outside our solar system. NASA put messages on the spacecraft. If aliens find one, the messages will tell them a little bit about Earth.

Pioneer 10 was launched in March 1972. It carried the first messages. Its first mission was to explore Jupiter. It holds an image of two humans. It also carries a map showing where Earth is in the solar system. *Pioneer 10* is now headed toward the star Aldebaran. If there are any aliens around there, they will have to wait about 2 million years to

THINK ABOUT IT

Imagine you are making a message to people on another planet. What sorts of things would you want them to know about Earth? It might help to think about what you would want to know about them.

After more than 30 years, NASA lost contact with *Pioneer 10* in 2002.

see *Pioneer 10*. That's how long it will take the probe to reach the star.

Voyager 1 launched in 1977. Its mission was to study planets and the deep solar system. It carries a golden record. On it are recordings of humans speaking and of music from around the world. *Voyager 1* passed Pluto in 1990. It will take the spacecraft 40,000 years to get close to another planet within our galaxy.

6.5 billion

Distance, in miles (10.5 billion km), separating Earth from *Voyager 1* in 1998, when it became the most distant man-made object ever.

- NASA has sent messages with some spacecraft in case aliens find them.
- The first was aboard *Pioneer 10* in 1972. It showed two humans and a map of Earth's solar system.
- The second message was aboard *Voyager 1*, the farthest man-made object in space.
- The most recent message was sent on *New Horizons*, which explored Pluto in 2015.

In 2015, *New Horizons* got a close-up look at Pluto.

The most recent message was sent off on the *New Horizons* probe. Regular people from around the world helped make the message. It includes many things, from well wishes in different languages to photos of a person's hometown. The ship's message can be updated. *New Horizons* passed Pluto in 2015. It will have enough power to send data back to Earth into the 2030s.

NASA Leads the Search for Life

The search for other life in the universe is one of the missions of NASA. The organization now believes life will be found somewhere. It's just a matter of when. They expect to find life within 20 years, possibly sooner.

One of the biggest reasons for this belief is water. NASA has used telescopes to find signs of water on many planets and asteroids. Jupiter, Saturn, and some of their moons have signs of water. Water is an essential part of life. These places also have signs of other components. One is energy, such as volcanic activity. Another is the presence of chemicals that are common in biology.

Another reason NASA believes life will be found soon is technology. NASA's spacecraft are able to detect planets far

Many scientists believe Jupiter's moon Europa has a saltwater ocean underneath its surface.

Astronauts have upgraded and serviced the Hubble Space Telescope on multiple missions.

from Earth. Each of these planets must be looked at closely to see whether life exists there. New telescopes are under construction that will be able to see even better.

NASA continues to look for signs of life both within our solar system and far beyond it.

1958
Year NASA was founded.

- Searching for alien life is one of NASA's main missions.
- NASA now believes proof of alien life will be found within 20 years.
- Signs of water on other planets is a good sign of possible life.
- Only further exploration will lead to the discovery of life.

Alien Life May Be Basic

Movies and television shows have often shown representations of aliens. They are often shown as smart creatures that may not be all that friendly. Intelligent life remains the focus of a lot of study. But it is likely any real discoveries of alien life will not look like science fiction.

Scientists are looking more for microbes. Microbes are tiny life-forms, including bacteria. But even though the life may be small, it would be a huge discovery. If simple life exists on one planet, it would make sense that there is more advanced life somewhere else. Astronomers are discovering more and more planets with the right conditions for life.

One key to finding these small life-forms could be found on Earth. Scientists are looking for extremophiles. These are life-forms that live in extreme conditions. Some of these have been found inside volcanoes. Temperatures on

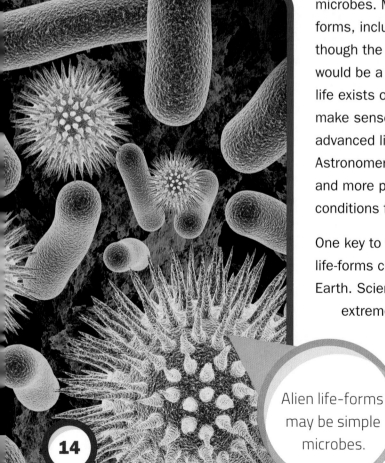

Alien life-forms may be simple microbes.

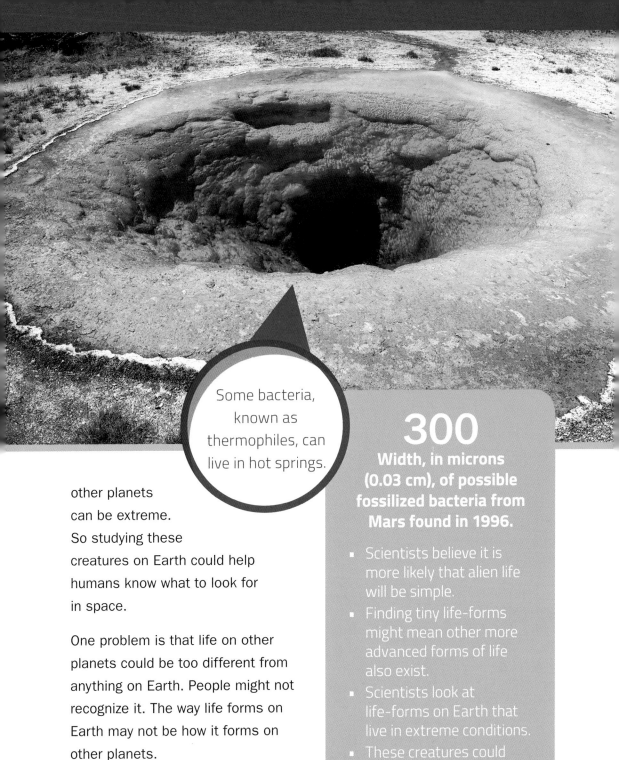

Some bacteria, known as thermophiles, can live in hot springs.

other planets can be extreme. So studying these creatures on Earth could help humans know what to look for in space.

One problem is that life on other planets could be too different from anything on Earth. People might not recognize it. The way life forms on Earth may not be how it forms on other planets.

300
Width, in microns (0.03 cm), of possible fossilized bacteria from Mars found in 1996.

- Scientists believe it is more likely that alien life will be simple.
- Finding tiny life-forms might mean other more advanced forms of life also exist.
- Scientists look at life-forms on Earth that live in extreme conditions.
- These creatures could help us understand how life survives on other planets.

Rovers Look for Martians

Beyond Earth, Mars is the next farthest planet from the sun. People have long thought Mars could have life on it. It has the next best climate in our solar system to support life. NASA has worked for decades on learning more about the red planet.

NASA landed its first spacecraft on Mars in 1976. The *Viking* landers sent back amazing pictures. But NASA could not tell whether any of the soil held life. NASA landed a rover on Mars in 1997. *Sojourner* allowed NASA to move around on Mars for the first time.

Spirit and *Opportunity* arrived in 2004. Both were able to find signs of ancient water. *Curiosity* is the latest Mars rover.

Curiosity has taken many soil samples from Mars.

GREAT *OPPORTUNITY*

Opportunity landed on Mars in 2004. It was supposed to study the surface for three months. But it was still going strong in May 2016. In March 2015, it surpassed the marathon distance of 26.2 miles (42.2 km) in its life. It has traveled farther on an off-Earth surface than any other machine.

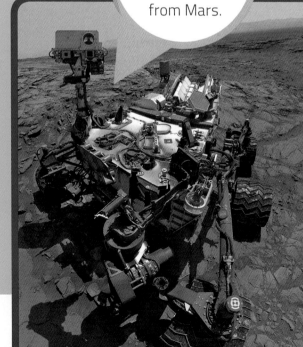

It has made several big discoveries. *Curiosity* has found several conditions for life in martian soil. It has found areas that once were soaked with water. It also has found chemicals that are present in living things.

Perhaps the biggest discovery came in 2015. NASA saw streaks of water on Mars. The streaks are not there all the time. This means water might only flow in warmer weather. The streaks are the best proof yet that water exists on Mars. That alone is reason to think life may not be far behind.

24:37
Length of a day on Mars, in hours and minutes. That is only slightly longer than Earth's day.

- Mars has similar conditions to Earth.
- Several spacecraft have landed on Mars since 1975.
- *Spirit* and *Opportunity* were able to find signs of ancient water.
- In 2015, NASA saw dark streaks indicating water still flows on Mars.

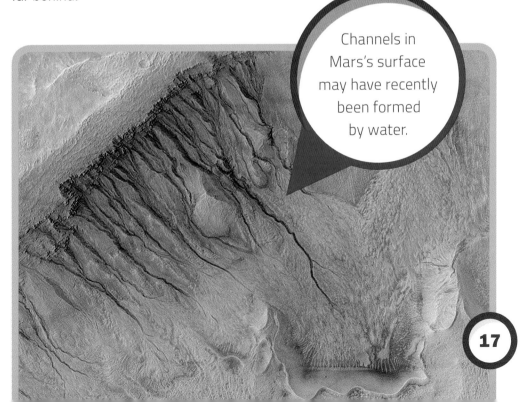

Channels in Mars's surface may have recently been formed by water.

Exoplanets Could Be Other Earths

So far, we know of only one planet that has life. That is Earth. Scientists have been looking for other planets that might be similar to Earth. An exoplanet is any planet that orbits a star other than the sun. Finding these planets is not easy. They are very, very far away. They also do not reflect much light.

But we can see the stars the planets go around. Scientists notice changes in the amount of light that reaches Earth. A change in the amount of light is a sign. It means something is passing in front of the star. Sometimes these objects are planets. Finding planets is the goal of the Kepler mission. *Kepler* launched in 2009. It orbits the sun looking for exoplanets.

Kepler can observe 100,000 stars at a time. It has found more than 1,000 planets.

As planets orbit stars, they can temporarily block light from reaching Earth.

Thousands more have yet to be confirmed. But only a few of the planets are in the "habitable zone" around stars. Planets within this distance from a star could possibly have liquid water. And water is one of the best indicators of life.

Kepler has found a few planets within the habitable zone. None match Earth's size and distance from a star. But there are hundreds of billions of stars. It could just be a matter of time before a close match is found.

Kepler launched aboard a rocket in 2009 with the mission of finding exoplanets.

$600 million
Cost of the *Kepler* spacecraft.

- An exoplanet is one that goes around a star other than our sun.
- *Kepler* searches for these planets.
- Planets in the habitable zone of a star could contain life.
- *Kepler* has found more than 1,000 planets.

KEPLER-452B

In 2015, NASA found one of the most Earth-like planets ever discovered. Kepler-452b is bigger and older than Earth. But it is about the same distance from its star as Earth is from the sun. The two planets have similar temperatures. But it will be hard to study Kepler-452b much further. The planet is more than 1,000 light-years from Earth.

NASA Hopes to Return Soil from Mars

Rovers such as *Curiosity* are important to understanding the soil on Mars. They are able to get an up-close look at the surface. They can dig up rocks and use sensors to see what they're made of. But there's only so much scientists can do from Earth. To see whether there's life on Mars, they need to see it for themselves.

By 2020, NASA hopes to launch a mission to Mars to bring back soil to Earth. Meteors that came from Mars have landed on Earth before. But scientists have never been able to study matter directly from the planet's surface. This would be a mission with multiple parts. A rover would first land on Mars and collect

Curiosity uses its drill to test whether it is a good place to take a sample.

WATER ON THE MOON

The moon might look pretty bare. But thanks to moon rocks brought back from Apollo missions, scientists may be changing that view. Traces of water have been found in some samples. Based on the age of the samples, it's possible the moon may once have had water on its surface.

soil. Unmanned rockets would then fly to Mars to pick up the soil and bring it to Earth.

NASA scientists would be able to test the soil up close. Much more is now known about the Moon because of the rocks NASA was able to study after landing there in the 1960s. Thanks to previous Mars landers, NASA knows which areas they want to take soil from.

It is not likely that the soil will come back with living creatures. But just in case, NASA will take special precautions. Other life-forms could be dangerous to humans. NASA

$1.9 billion

Estimated cost of the Mars 2020 mission.

- Current Mars rovers can perform some tests on martian soil.
- Scientists could better test Mars's soil on Earth.
- NASA is planning an unmanned mission to collect soil samples from Mars in 2020.

will check the soil to make sure it is safe. Then it will release the samples to be tested.

Curiosity's first soil scoop mark on Mars

Manned Mission to Mars: The Next Giant Leap

Mars has been heavily studied. It has been observed from Earth. Rovers have explored the martian surface. As a result, scientists know a lot about the red planet. NASA believes the planet has the most potential for signs of life in our solar system. But to truly examine it up close, people will have to travel there.

NASA hopes to send astronauts to Mars by the 2030s. It is already prepping for the long journey. NASA sends humans to the International Space Station (ISS). Going to the

Astronaut Scott Kelly finished a yearlong stay on the International Space Station in 2016.

THINK ABOUT IT

What do you think are the biggest challenges of the long trip to Mars? What do you think astronauts will do along the way? What would you bring with you on the trip?

ISS gets astronauts used to spending time in space. NASA hopes to land astronauts on an asteroid in the 2020s. This will prepare them for landing and taking samples on Mars.

If humans do reach Mars, one concern is that humans may bring organisms with them.

In 2015, NASA discovered places on Mars where water might be flowing. This would be an important place for astronauts to explore. But finding alien life is only one concern about a mission to Mars. Another is accidentally bringing life to Mars. Germs from Earth could ride with the astronauts. They could contaminate Mars. Scientists do not know what would happen if germs from Earth contacted life on Mars.

Rovers and other machines can be cleaned with chemicals and heat. Human astronauts would be much harder to clean. So the places humans would most want to explore might be off-limits. We would not want to ruin any hopes of finding life through the process of looking for it.

7
Months it would take for a manned spacecraft to get to Mars.

- Sending humans to Mars is the last step in exploring the planet.
- Humans would be able to search for life better than robots can.
- NASA hopes to send people to Mars by the 2030s.
- Germs from Earth might pose a risk to any life on Mars.

Bigger Telescopes Might Spot Life

Telescopes in space can see better than those on Earth. They are above the atmosphere, which can distort light coming from space. The Hubble Space Telescope was launched in 1990. It has been making discoveries ever since. But a new telescope soon will outdo it.

The James Webb Space Telescope is scheduled to launch in 2018.

The telescope cost $8.8 billion to make. It will be more powerful than Hubble and more than twice the size. It will be about the size of a tennis court. The telescope will travel much farther into space than Hubble.

Not only will the Webb see

The Webb Telescope will use 18 hexagonal mirrors to gather light from deep in space.

exoplanets; it will also study their atmospheres. It will be able to sense whether they have liquid water. It also will be able to study how planets form. Knowing a planet's past can tell us about whether it ever had life on it.

In the future, telescopes will be even better. A telescope five times bigger than Hubble could view the planets detected by the Kepler mission. Such a telescope could be in space by the 2030s.

The Webb Telescope will allow scientists to get a closer look at distant galaxies.

24

Distance, in miles (39 km), from which the Webb Telescope can see a penny.

- Telescopes in space can be very large and can see distant objects.
- The Hubble Space Telescope has been in space for more than 25 years.
- The James Webb Space Telescope will be bigger and better than Hubble.
- The Webb Telescope will study Earth-like planets for signs of life.

THINK ABOUT IT

There are some objects close enough that we can see them without a telescope. What objects can you see in the night sky? How many planets do you think you can see?

The Chemical Laptop Is a Space Laboratory

Until humans can bring back soil from other planets, we will have to study it remotely. It's important to have the best tools for this task. Scientists have created something they call the "chemical laptop." It looks like a normal laptop computer, but much thicker. When launched, it would be the most advanced testing system ever to leave Earth. It's a full-scale lab made small.

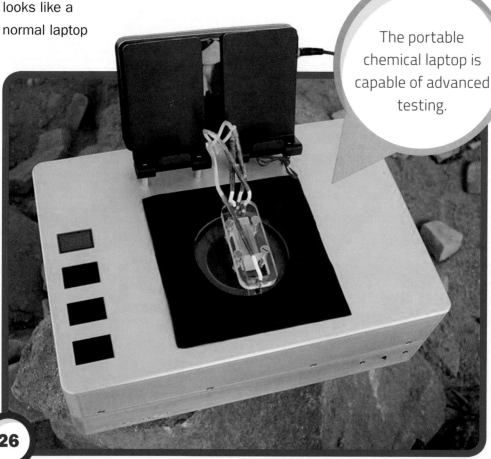

The portable chemical laptop is capable of advanced testing.

212

Temperature, in degrees Fahrenheit (100°C), that the chemical laptop can heat objects to.

- The best way to test samples from space is in a lab on Earth.
- Today, scientists can test samples only remotely.
- The chemical laptop could someday test matter while on another planet.
- The laptop searches for chemicals found in living things.

The chemical laptop will allow scientists to do lab tests remotely.

The laptop tests matter for chemicals common to life. In order to test something, the sample must contain liquid. This could prove difficult when dealing with ice. But the laptop is able to melt samples. The liquid is then drawn into the laptop. From there, the laptop looks for acids found in life-forms. These acids can also be found in nonliving things. But the laptop will be able to tell the difference.

NASA has tested the laptop on Earth. It was attached to a model rover. In 2017, NASA plans to test it in the cold, dry Atacama Desert in Chile. The conditions would be similar to those on Mars. The laptop would work together with the rover. The rover would take samples. Then the laptop would test them.

In space exploration, lighter and smaller is better. The chemical laptop could make one part of searching for alien life easier.

Fact Sheet

- Starting in the late 1950s, the United States and the Soviet Union competed to see which country could put a person into space. The Soviets sent the first person, Yuri Gagarin, to space in April 1961.

- One of the most notable achievements in space history was the landing of humans on the moon in 1969.

- NASA launched the first space shuttle in 1981. Space shuttles were reusable and flew for 30 years.

- It wasn't until 1992 that planets beyond our solar system were discovered. Two scientists discovered two planets in the constellation Virgo. Because of high levels of radiation, they knew right away these planets couldn't sustain life.

- The 100-Year Starship project was announced in 2010. It is a joint operation of the US Department of Defense and NASA. The project aims to bring the necessary groups together to make deep-space travel possible within 100 years.

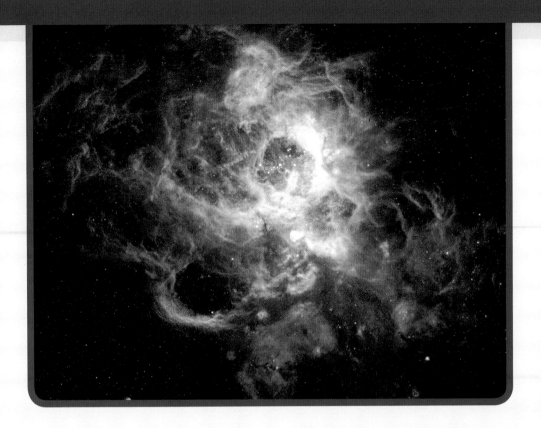

- A significant discovery of possible martian life was made in 1996. Scientists were analyzing a meteorite that had come from Mars. Under a microscope, it looked as if there was a fossil of bacteria. If true, it would have been the first sign of other life in the universe. Since then, scientists have come to disagree on whether or not it came from a living creature. Given signs of water on Mars, it remains possible it came from a living creature.

- While SETI's work continues, world-famous physicist Stephen Hawking has launched his own initiative. In 2015, Hawking announced the Breakthrough Listen initiative. The 10-year project will collect huge amounts of data by using many radio telescopes around the world. Hawking's search will have 50 times more detail and will cover 10 times more of the sky than other searches to date. It is one of the most serious efforts to date at finding alien life.

Glossary

antenna
A piece of metal used for receiving radio waves.

asteroid
An object smaller than a planet that orbits a larger object.

astronomer
A person who studies and makes observations about space.

atmosphere
The air and gases that surround a planet.

canal
A man-made river or stream.

climate
The weather typical of a place over a long period of time.

contaminate
To introduce harmful or undesirable substances.

light-year
The distance that light travels in one year, about 5.88 trillion miles (9.46 trillion km).

meteor
A piece of matter that enters Earth's atmosphere.

orbit
To travel in a circular path around something.

precaution
Something done in advance to prevent something bad from happening.

telescope
A device used for seeing far distances.

For More Information

Books

Aguilar, David. *Alien Worlds: Your Guide to Extraterrestrial Life.* Washington, DC: National Geographic, 2013.

Aguilar, David. *Space Encyclopedia: A Tour of Our Solar System and Beyond.* Washington, DC: National Geographic, 2013.

Carlson, Mary Kay. *Beyond the Solar System: Exploring Galaxies, Black Holes, Alien Planets, and More.* Chicago: Chicago Review Press, 2013.

Visit 12StoryLibrary.com

Scan the code or use your school's login at **12StoryLibrary.com** for recent updates about this topic and a full digital version of this book. Enjoy free access to:

- Digital ebook
- Breaking news updates
- Live content feeds
- Videos, interactive maps, and graphics
- Additional web resources

Note to educators: Visit 12StoryLibrary.com/register to sign up for free premium website access. Enjoy live content plus a full digital version of every 12-Story Library book you own for every student at your school.

Index

Aldebaran, 10–11
Allen Telescope Array
   (ATA), 9

chemical laptop, 26–27
Cocconi, Giuseppe, 6
Curiosity, 17, 20

Drake, Frank, 6
Drake Equation, 6–7

exoplanet, 18–19,
   24–25

Hubble Space Telescope,
   12, 24–25

International Space
   Station (ISS), 22

James Webb Space
   Telescope, 24–25
Jupiter, 10, 12

Kepler, 18–19, 25
Kepler-452b, 19

Mars, 4, 16–17, 20–23,
   27
Milky Way galaxy, 6
Morrison, Philip, 6

National Aeronautics and
   Space Administration
   (NASA), 7, 10, 12–13,
   16–17, 19, 20–23, 27
New Horizons, 11

Opportunity, 16–17

Pathfinder, 16
Pioneer 10, 10–11
Pluto, 11

radio telescope, 8–9
Roswell, New Mexico, 5

Saturn, 12
Search for
   Extraterrestrial
   Intelligence (SETI),
   6–9
Sojourner, 16
Spirit, 17

telescope (optical), 4, 8,
   24–25

unidentified flying object
   (UFO), 5

Viking, 16
Voyager 1, 11

War of the Worlds, 4

About the Author

Todd Kortemeier is a writer from Minneapolis, Minnesota. He is a graduate of the University of Minnesota's School of Journalism & Mass Communication. He has authored many books for young people.